P9-DDP-361

UNLEASHED

LIVE THE BALANCED, CENTERED, AND SEXY LIFE YOU DESERVE

DIANA ANTHOLIS

UNLEASHED
Live the Balanced, Centered, and Sexy Life You Deserve

Copyright © 2013 Diana Antholis

All rights reserved. No part of this book may be reproduced, scanned, or distributed in any printed or electronic form without permission.

Author Photography: Lora Warnick
lorawarnick.com

Cover Design: Steven Antholis
svenom.com

ISBN-13: 978-0-615-89223-8

This book is dedicated to all of us who want to feel
balanced, centered, and sexy.

Please consult your physician before attempting any exercises to be sure you are cleared for fitness activities presented within this book, on DianaAntholis.com, and any additional social networks associated with Diana Antholis.

All matters regarding physical and mental health should be supervised by a health practitioner knowledgeable in treating that particular condition.

If you have chosen not to consult a health practitioner, you acknowledge you are participating at your own risk.

The author shall not be liable or responsible for any loss, injury, or damage allegedly arising from any information or suggestion in this book.

CONTENTS

"Your life yields to the thoughts of your mind and the actions you take. The goal is to be so in tune with your essence, your intuition and your heart that this connection becomes the driving force in your life. When you are connected to your essence you are connected to the energy of the greater whole and will be guided towards greatness. When you trust yourself and express with heartfelt conviction that which you really are, you flip the script on whatever is lacking in your life and draw it to you automatically."

—JACKSON KIDDARD

PREFACE

Happiness.

We want it. We chase it. We aspire to it. We wonder how to get it, where it comes from, and how to make it last. We think external things, circumstances, or people give us happiness; but that's only temporary.

True happiness comes from within.

Because that's all we really want—to be happy.
To live life on our own terms.
To feel good.
To exude confidence.
To have the guts to go for anything we want.
To start...and to finish.
To regain control.
To be healthy.
To feel like ourselves.
To feel comfortable, confident, and sexy in our own skin.
To be who we really are.

After 10 years of letting my body be overtaken by stress, I can finally say that I know how to regain control. This wasn't an overnight fix (obviously). It took hard work, and I still focus on my well-being every single day. But I'm here to tell you that you can absolutely live the life you want (in a much shorter period of time).

INTRODUCTION

MY STORY

Ten years ago, my digestive system flipped my life upside down and backwards. I became sick every time I ate. And no one knew what was wrong.

After meetings and tests with three different doctors over four years, it seemed as though my case was hopeless. Prescriptions didn't work. Supplements only masked the problem. Natural remedies helped but did not cure me.

No one could get to the core of the problem. They only looked at the symptoms and how to alleviate them, which often resulted in temporary fixes.

So, I continued to suffer. I had good days and bad days; but when my pain started to severely alter my everyday life, I couldn't take it anymore. Simple pleasures and exciting events turned into major anxieties. I never knew when my uncomfortable symptoms would hit. I lived in fear of getting sick and had to do something about it.

When I attended graduate school, I reached my breaking point. I started doing research online to figure out how to fix my digestive issues. I knew that stress was exacerbating my symptoms, but I didn't know how to get to the core problem.

I learned how to eat and in what order to eat certain foods to help my intestines process food better. I completed a 100-day program that allowed me to completely relax for 30 minutes every day.

This all helped tremendously. I started feeling normal again; but whenever extreme stress happened in my life, I reverted right back to being sick.

At this point, I had been dealing with severe digestive issues for nine years. It started in 2002, my second year of college, and continued through working in New York City and San Diego, attending graduate school in Washington D.C. in 2009, and starting my own business in 2010.

In the summer of 2011, I randomly came across a blog by Abigail Steidley that talked about how stress in our minds can manifest as physical pain. I read more, downloaded the resources, and became enlightened by this subject. Dr. John Sarno, of the book *The Mindbody Prescription*, really opened my mind to the possibility that the pain I was experiencing in my intestines was a direct result of the thoughts and emotions I was experiencing in my brain (or, rather, the thoughts and emotions that my brain was hiding from me—thereby creating physical pain).

Because of the science and research behind mind-body syndromes, my logical side was thrilled. I did more research on mind-body syndromes and studied how this could be applied to so many different facets of life. It wasn't only for people with digestive problems; it was for people who were looking to lose weight, resolve back pain, relieve migraines, and more.

I took a course on how to work directly with mind-body syndromes so I could help myself, but also help my clients. I saw they were going through the same exact thing. Thoughts and emotions were being suppressed and causing us all harm in the form of digestive issues, migraines, and weight gain. Everyone manifests mind-body syndromes differently, but the problems are all the same at their cores.

After conducting the major exercises and coaching principles on myself, I started to feel better. My digestive issues were becoming fewer to nearly non-existent. I brought up feelings from the past and dealt with them. I kept a daily journal writing down every single thought and feeling I was having, no matter how upsetting or embarrassing. I dealt with my feelings, which is something I didn't do ten years ago—something that had been causing me physical pain for so long.

I started applying these concepts to my coaching clients and was beyond thrilled and amazed when they were getting the same results that I did. They started pushing through their self-imposed limitations, recalling events from the past that had hindered them for years. They started sleeping better, eating healthier, beginning exercise programs, losing weight, standing up for themselves, accepting themselves, and believing that they could do what they wanted. And more than that, they stayed that way as long as they were always in touch with their thoughts and feelings…as long as they were always aware and in touch with themselves.

This is powerful stuff.

The most fascinating part is that I feel so normal, so much like myself now, that I can hardly remember those ten years of torture. Don't get me wrong, I surely won't forget that time, but I don't actively remember it. I don't think about my past. I focus on my present and near future.

My digestive woes are slim to none. I'm not perfect, nor is anyone. I am not completely stress-free, but I know now how to handle it. I realize I have control. I don't let it completely take over my body anymore. I have the tools to fight.

I use these tools every day. It's not exhausting; it's become part of me. I'm thankful for it. I have an awareness of my mind and body that I'm proud of and, because of that, I can live my best life. I'm happy. I'm healthy. I feel incredible.

As I enter a new decade of my life, I've never felt more
confident and comfortable with myself.

My journey—my struggles, my pain, and my happiness—
has inspired me to share what I know with you. We may not
have the same physical situations, but I understand the
challenges of feeling disconnected with your body and your
mind.

You are stuck. You feel uncomfortable. You are sad. You
are stressed. You feel panicked. You are lacking confidence.
You feel as though you've lost control. You are scared. You are
worried. You don't feel like yourself—and that pisses you off.

I dedicate this book to you. You can live a balanced life.
You can feel centered amid the chaos. You can feel sexy.

These next chapters will take you through the exercises and
tools I use to live my best life. I actively use them with my
clients, my friends, and myself. I'm determined to help those
who need it and who want to feel fantastic.

The three key mantras of this book and my business sum
up my entire philosophy:

DEFINE YOUR BALANCE

Balance is what you want it to be. Don't let people tell you that
you can't have it or that it doesn't exist. It's what you make of
it. It's how you want to live your life. Balance is completely
subjective and you can find yours.

In Chapters One and Two, we will talk about living a life
you love and focusing on what lights your fire.

FIND YOUR CENTER

Centering yourself means observing your thoughts. You are not
your thoughts. Repeat. You are not your thoughts. But you can
become your thoughts. Big difference. You have control. Take
yourself out of your brain and observe. Start thinking the way
you want to be thinking.

In Chapter Three, we discuss the concept that you can rule your thoughts and believe in your sexy. In Chapter Four, I take you through my most effective coaching exercise to shift your mindset and create your own mantra to achieve inner peace in a matter of minutes.

UNLEASH YOUR SEXY

Confidence. Power. You have it in you. Being aware of your mind and body is sexy. Being healthy is sexy. Exercising is sexy. Being you is sexy. Accepting yourself is sexy. Living the life you want is sexy.

In Chapter Five, I share the secrets to exuding confidence. In Chapter Six, we indulge your mind, body, and soul. In Chapter Seven, you fully accept your inner sexy. In Chapter Eight, you own your evolution through accountability. In Chapter Nine, you nourish your body with food swaps that still gratify your taste buds but are much healthier, foods you can eat every day and every week for optimum health, and how many servings of the food groups you should be having every day. In Chapter Ten, you fall in love with movement. I teach you my tricks to get you exercising in a short amount of time, plus offer bonus workout videos.

These philosophies are covered in depth in the following chapters, explaining what they are, what I went through, and how to take action.

HOW TO USE THIS GUIDE

Every chapter has written exercises so you can take action and use this guide in a practical manner. I recommend using the guide as follows:

- Start reading the guide. Feel free to start on the section that is a priority for you.

- If you feel compelled to stop and complete an exercise right away, then please do so!

- If you would like to read the entire guide and then go back in and complete the exercises, I have provided a list of all exercises at the end of this book so you can choose which ones you would like to dive into first.

- Take your time with each exercise and have fun writing down your answers.

- Take a break when you need one. This guide is full of powerful information that is going to help you live your best life. Focus, breathe, and enjoy the ride.

CHAPTER ONE

LIVE A LIFE YOU LOVE

"Often people attempt to live their lives backwards: they try to have more things, or more money, in order to do more of what they want so they will be happier. The way it actually works is the reverse. You must first be who you really are, then, do what you need to do, in order to have what you want."
—MARGARET YOUNG

I believe in balance. I don't believe that it's a single, straight, horizontal line. Dedicating equal energy to every single aspect of your life is not necessary. Every relationship or responsibility does not require your fullest attention.

Balance is subjective. A company can't define it for you. Your boss can't define it for you. Your spouse can't define it for you. Only you can define it for yourself. So, what does balance mean to you?

Work/life balance exists only if you want it to. If you don't want it to or don't think it can happen, then it doesn't exist. If you believe that you can live life on your own terms, dedicate the time you want to what you want, and have a work life that does not trump your personal life, then work/life balance does exist.

Do you live to work or work to live? There is no right answer. It's up to you; but if you're reading this book right now, chances are you want to work to live.

You want to appreciate life more. You want to have energizing experiences. You want to feel good about your present life and where it is headed in the future. You want to be proud of yourself. You want to be able to talk about your life with a smile on your face.

Work is a big part of life, obviously. Some people see it as a sense of purpose. Some people see it as a paycheck. Some people see it as a means to have other life experiences. It's important that you understand how you view your work in order to define your own balance.

WORK/LIFE BALANCE EXERCISE:

Answer the following questions:

1. Do you work to live?

2. Do you live to work?

3. How do you feel about your current job?

4. How do you feel about the time you spend at work?

5. Does the amount of time that you spend on your work and your personal life make you happy?

6. When someone asks you what you do for work, how do you respond? (Pay attention next time to your tone of voice and your body language. Does the other person get excited or dismayed when you talk about your job?)

By answering these questions, you will get a sense of how you feel about your work/life. Now answer this: How do you feel?

After thinking about—and writing down—your thoughts on work and life, do you feel stressed? Overwhelmed? Sad? Angry? Happy? Fulfilled?

Write down your feelings and hold on to what you wrote. Remember, work/life balance is about what matters to you. It's about your priorities. It's about YOU.

DEFINING WORK/LIFE ON YOUR OWN TERMS

"How you think about a problem is more important than the problem itself—so always think positively."
—NORMAN VINCENT PEALE

Now that you can see what your work/life looks like, would you like to change anything? Are you happy with your current status? If not, what do you need to do so that you feel more balanced?

What does your ideal life look like? Let's think about your ideal day. Take the time to think about, or write down, how you envision your ideal day.

For example, here's what I would like mine to look like right now:

Mornings: Wake up naturally and start my day by eating a great breakfast followed by some yoga. Block 2-3 hours to work on a project or client meetings.

Afternoons: Take a 1-2 hour break for lunch and exercise. Block 2-3 hours for projects and clients.

Evenings: Work on a hobby, go out and be social, and read before bed.

Does this mean that every day will follow the schedule I've outlined? No. Would I be able to do this every day with conducting coaching and exercise sessions, and participating in other activities? No.

This is my ideal day, and there is no reason why I can't have this day more often than not. In this schedule, I have prioritized what is important to me and blocked off time for it. I chunked time for my projects and clients. I gave myself breaks when I know I'll need them. I gave myself a good chunk of time for a hobby in the evening to unwind and relax.

Of course things will deviate from this schedule and that's okay. But having some sort of structure really helps you get things done. Today, I specifically blocked off a two-hour chunk just for writing. Then, I will take a break for lunch and exercise, work on a client project for another two-hour block, and relax for the rest of the evening.

Fellow entrepreneurs, you know that you can get a full day's worth of work done in three hours. Shut off those email notifications, remove sounds on your phone, and forbid yourself from checking Facebook. It works. All of my notifications are off right now. When you chunk your time and focus, you will be amazed by all the work you can get done.

If you are in an office from 9am-5pm, this still works. How many times do you get stuck in unproductive meetings, dragged into projects that come out of nowhere, or interrupted by coworkers or phone calls? Too often. When I worked in advertising, this was the story of my life. To combat the distractions, when I arrived in the office (or even the night before), I made a list of what I needed to get done and allocated time in between meetings to work only on specific projects. Yes, I was interrupted. No, I didn't always finish everything on my list. But it was a starting point in getting things done.

Always, always schedule time for breaks. I would eat lunch at my desk, and I know most of you do too. I still find myself eating lunch in front of my computer. We have a false sense of urgency that we must stay at our desks in case a critical email comes through or an important client calls. Get outside. Go for a walk. Get up for five minutes during the day and take your eyes off the computer. I know how you feel. I used to spend 12 hours in front of a computer in the office and that hasn't changed much now that I work for myself. After hours of time spent online, we can start to lose our minds. It doesn't have to be like that.

IDEAL DAY EXERCISE:

Write out your ideal day. Block off times for projects, clients, meetings, breaks, and fun. It doesn't have to be an hourly schedule, but certainly feel free to make it that way if you want. It won't be perfect. I don't want you to be perfect. But staying somewhat within the structure will make you feel more accomplished and productive.

You can start how I did with breaking the day into mornings, afternoons, and evenings. Just start to put your must-dos and want-to-dos down on paper in some kind of organized fashion.

CHAPTER 2

FOCUS ON WHAT LIGHTS YOUR FIRE

"Prioritize, plan, and execute your week's tasks based on
importance rather than urgency."
—STEPHEN COVEY

What are your priorities? What matters to you? There is much
debate over what work/life balance means. People have even
introduced new terms: flexibility, integration, fit, merge. Using
these terms in lieu of "balance" is just semantics. Ultimately,
balance is about doing what you want to do during your day
and in your life.

Now that you've designed your ideal day, look at what you
put in there. Those are your priorities. Did you schedule time
for lunch? A walk? The gym? Drinks with friends? Reading
your favorite book? Go back and review your ideal day. Does
anything need to be added? Subtracted? Your ideal day can
change, as needed.

Your priorities can stay consistent or change each day. You
may want to take a walk every morning, but you may only want
to have drinks with friends once a week. Remember that you
are in control of your priorities. You have the choice in doing
yoga three times per week, walking twice per week, and doing a
spin class once per week. Your schedule doesn't have to be
fancy; it has to fit the life you want.

PRIORITIES EXERCISE:

Answer the following questions:

1. What's important to you? What are your priorities? What are the must-haves in your life?

2. Can you have it in your life? Can you have this thing/activity in your life? Yes or No.

3. Are you willing to take the time to put it in your life? Will you have a conversation with yourself and allow yourself to set aside time for your priority? Yes or No.

4. Do you deserve to have it in your life? This is the big one. Do you deserve it? Are you worthy of it? Yes or No.

If you answered "yes" to the last three questions, then I want to hear a resounding "hell yeah!" and see you incorporate your priorities into your life—no matter what they are.

If you answered "no" to any of the questions, what's stopping you? Why can't you have it? Why can't you take the time? Why don't you deserve it? Think about it. Why?

Seriously answer those questions. You may find the answers sound silly when you say them out loud or put them on paper.

Exercising has always been a priority for me. However, when I was working 12-14 hour days in an office, finding time to exercise was really hard. I'm not a morning person, so the three total times I got up early to go to the gym before work was torture. After work, I would have to fight to leave early enough to make it to a gym class.

During graduate school, I was so overwhelmed with all the work I had to do that I completely stopped exercising. Huge mistake! I somehow convinced myself that I didn't have time to exercise. School was on my mind 24/7 and taking time away from studying seemed like a terrible idea. Yet, spending even just 30 minutes a day exercising would have helped me tenfold.

People think that being an entrepreneur gives you all the time in the world to have a great life balance. Reality: most of the women I work with are entrepreneurs or freelancers who don't have a structured schedule. When you have more time, it's harder to organize it. You think you always have time to do something, so you push it off. Then you get nothing done. I've found that sometimes I don't give myself enough time for exercise, so I will literally drop everything I'm doing and take the time to exercise if I haven't planned it. It recharges me and is never a waste of time. Taking care of you should always be your top priority.

HOW TO INTEGRATE YOUR PRIORITIES

Time, time, time. We never seem to have enough time. Most things take much less time than you think. Let's use exercising as an example. I know what happens when you think about exercising. Your thought process goes something like this:

> "Tomorrow, I'm going to exercise."
> Tomorrow now becomes today.
> You wake up too late. "Okay, I'll go to the gym at lunch or after work."
> Lunch comes and goes. "I'll go after work."
> The end of the workday comes. "So tired, so hungry."
> Or you were at work late and when it's time to go home you say to yourself, "No time to do a workout. Must eat and go to bed."
> You get in bed. "Tomorrow, I'm going to exercise."
> *And the cycle continues.*

Here's the thing. All you need is 30 minutes per day to exercise. If you can do more, fabulous. But on days that you are really pressed for time, when you wake up late, and/or work late, you can absolutely carve out 30 minutes for physical activity. You don't need a gym. You just need some space on the floor in your home.

Bonus: The exercises section of this book contains a website address that gives you access to two external workout videos that can be done in 30 minutes.

Integrating your priorities into your life can happen easily if you structure your day. Go back to your ideal day. Once you start living a more structured life, commit to your schedule. No matter what you are doing, stop and do what you have planned for yourself. There have been times when I wanted to keep working through the breaks I gave myself. Sometimes it's good if you are really feeling the energy and are on fire. But most of the time, you will work yourself tired or hungry and then become cranky and we all know that being tired, hungry, and cranky is not fun.

Stop working. Take the break. Follow your schedule until it comes naturally.

ME TIME EXERCISE:

1. Write down a list of all the things that you would love to do every day: personal or professional.
   Examples: Reading a chapter from your favorite book in the morning, focusing on a specific project for two hours per day, making dinner at home, walking one mile, etc.

2. Pick one thing on that list to do every day for the next four days.

Why four days? There is science behind the fact that after four days, your brain believes that you *do* something. If you do something once, you tell others that you've done it once. If you do something twice, you tell others you've done it a couple of times. If you do something three times, you tell others you've done it a few times. If you do something four times, you tell others it's something you do. Think about it.

The idea is to keep adding to the list every four days, but to start small. So by the time a few months go by, you will have formed new habits doing the things you've always wanted to do everyday.

But you must do this one thing every single day for four days. Create the habit. Reward yourself for sticking to it. (This is a favorite exercise of my clients. It works!)

TIME VERSUS THOUGHT MANAGEMENT

While talking with a client about her overwhelming stress at work, I realized that it was neither a time management issue nor an organization issue. Yes, scheduling and being aware of your time and being organized are incredibly important. But what she really needed was thought management.

She was letting her thoughts totally take over her mind and body. She was on the verge of tears, if not already crying, every time I talked to her about this. She felt that everyone else was ahead of her, that they had their act together, that they magically were able to get projects done without any distractions, and that they could automatically keep on top of all their emails while organizing their projects accordingly.

She felt embarrassed, ashamed, and stupid for having so much work to do, having to ask for help and accept help, and for not keeping up with her workload.

After discussing prioritization techniques like chunking and focusing on one project at a time, I realized that all of those techniques were just covering up the real problem. She needed to get a handle on her thoughts.

If you continuously say all of these negative things to yourself, you will continue in your downward spiral. Nothing will get done. Work will pile up and you will continue to feel sorry for yourself. That's no way to live.

"The key is to trust your nonverbal, felt experience. If a thought causes suffering, it isn't true."
—MARTHA BECK

HOW TO GET OUT OF YOUR THOUGHTS

Start thinking differently. Here is how:

Write down your accomplishments. The biggest and the littlest things. Finished the presentation for tomorrow? Write it down. Wrote back someone who has been emailing you every day? Write it down. Ate lunch outside of the office? Write it down. (Yes, that is an accomplishment! You know it!) By writing down everything you've already done, you will feel better about your day. You will realize that you have done much more than you originally thought and you will feel extremely productive. Start making the list now.

Recognize that everyone needs help. That's why we work in teams. That's why there are big companies with many departments with many employees. What can you delegate? What can you ask for help with? Who can you go to when you need something? Explain your situation and people will help you.

Start being grateful for what you do have. This particular client I was talking about earlier said that her boyfriend was willing to help her with some projects—work and personal. She had wanted to see him that night but told him of her situation and stress. He offered his help. When she talked to me after that, she said she was so embarrassed that she even needed his help! I told her she needed to shift her mindset and think instead about how incredibly awesome it is that she has a man in her life who is willing to help her. Reframe your situation.

TIME AND THOUGHT MANAGEMENT EXERCISE:

If you have found yourself in a similar situation, here's how to navigate it:

1. Time Management 101: Write down everything you did all day, preferably by every 30 minutes. Notice where you are wasting your time. (You'll be surprised by how much time you spend checking Facebook or swiping your phone.)

2. Create a schedule that prioritizes your work, tasks, email, social media, food, exercise, and fun. You do not always need to follow the schedule exactly, but it's good to have it in place so your days don't end up being wasted by looking at videos online and replying to emails that can wait. Save the videos and articles you find in a separate folder to look at later when you have free time. (My favorite tool is Pocket: gctpocket.com)

3. Reframe your thoughts. Get that nasty voice telling you that you aren't good enough, smart enough, productive enough, fast enough, or promotable enough out of your head. That voice is bringing you down. It's not you. I have a special technique I use on myself and on others when that voice nags you incessantly.

SCHEDULING YOUR THOUGHTS (BONUS TECHNIQUE):

When I was going through the break-up from a long relationship, I did a lot of processing, thinking, and feeling. I read one article that, surprisingly, really helped (because break-up articles are rarely helpful, in my opinion). It was by Christine Hassler on The Daily Love. She said that when you start thinking about your ex, or are feeling really terrible about the break-up, tell yourself that you have only one time during the day to think about it.

So you would say to yourself, "Okay I'm only allowed to think about him/her at 5pm today for 10 minutes." Whenever the thoughts pop up into your mind during the day, you tell yourself that you are not allowed to think about it now and that it must wait until later. Then, two things can happen:

You only take the 10 minutes to grieve, cry, punch something, etc. and have a much better day not thinking about your ex.

-or-

You completely forget about your scheduled break-up thoughts time.

Honestly, when I first read that, I thought it was nonsense. How could that possibly work? Until I tried it. I found myself completely forgetting to think about my ex during that scheduled time. I would go through the day with random thoughts popping into my mind, telling myself that I was not allowed to think about it right then, that I must wait until later on. It totally worked. The thoughts became fewer and fewer.

I took this technique and applied it to the stress we feel in daily life. Because we've talked about how the main culprit of our work/life frustrations is most likely not time management, but rather thought management, I want you to give yourself one time during the day when you are allowed to feel sorry for yourself, overwhelmed, or embarrassed.

When you let yourself think these things throughout the day, you become these thoughts. When you push them out of your head, tell yourself to do your work, and set a time to think about how badly you feel about yourself later, you'll find that you'll end up feeling better about yourself because you actually did what you set out to do.

And it's also a bit ridiculous to schedule time to feel sorry for yourself. Agreed?

I woke up one morning with this conundrum. I was getting angry with myself for not writing part of this book by the time I wanted to. I woke up, did 15 minutes of yoga, sat in front of my computer without checking email or social media, and started writing. I was so proud of myself for getting my work done.

Remember, it all starts in your head. You are not your thoughts. You are the observer. You can control what you think and how you feel.

CHAPTER 3

RULE YOUR THOUGHTS & BELIEVE IN YOUR SEXY

"No one can create negativity or stress within you. Only you
can do that by virtue of how you process your world."
—WAYNE DYER

Stress is a cover emotion. What does that mean? It means stress
is the umbrella that's covering up whatever emotion you are
truly feeling. Most likely, the emotion is anger, sadness, or fear.

YOUR BRAIN

Our brains are wired to have a basic emergency plan when
faced with a threatening situation: fight or flight. Back in the
day, this made sense as we were surrounded by danger. (Think:
lion coming to chase you, hunting for your food, etc.) That
type of danger rarely happens now, but our brains still operate
in much the same way.

When you encounter a fear-based thought surrounding
your job, your brain automatically goes into fight or flight mode
and increases your stress hormones. This happens because you
believe your stressed-out thoughts. Your sympathetic nervous
system is on high alert, which causes tension, negative
emotions, and even pain and illness.

YOUR BODY

Our bodies react to stress physically. These physical signs are created by hormones and adrenaline. When in fight or flight mode, physical symptoms can come in many forms: muscle tension, digestive distress, muscle contractions, loss of oxygen, glucose overproduction, and/or crippling pain. This happens because when we are at high alert, our blood flows away from our intestines and skin. When we are resting and digesting, our blood flow returns to our organs.

Many times, we believe that something is structurally wrong with us when we feel pain, so we go from doctor to doctor trying to figure out what is wrong. If there is nothing wrong, it can be attributed to being in a constant state of fight or flight. When you are in this state, your body cannot heal. You are susceptible to more illness because your immunities are lower.

YOU ARE NOT YOUR THOUGHTS

"The components of anxiety, stress, fear, and anger do not exist independently of you in the world. They simply do not exist in the physical world, even though we talk about them as if they do."
—WAYNE DYER

Thoughts are not physical, but they can create physical reactions in the body. The left hemisphere of the brain is the logical, practical part. It is generally dominant. It judges, it analyzes, it compares, it is responsible for the "what ifs," it connects the past, present, and future, and it pieces together information to form stories. Here's the problem: the stories aren't always correct. In fact, they can be big fat lies. The left hemisphere can't distinguish between fact and fiction.

That's where your right hemisphere comes in. It's your intuition, the big picture, the part of your brain responsible for deep inner peace, love, joy, compassion, truth, visions, empathy, and living in the moment. (Doesn't that all sound wonderful?)

Now, all you have to do is create a balance. Ha! Easier said than done.

Your left, judging, analyzing hemisphere is most-likely dominant. So all of those thoughts spewing out of it win over your right hemisphere.

Unfortunately, these thoughts can be destructive because they cause us to question, compare, and criticize ourselves. This causes stress and anxiety-inducing emotions. (Remember, these are cover emotions for fear, anger, sadness, etc.)

The key is to access your intuition, your gut feeling, that voice in your head or that feeling in your heart that tells you exactly what to do. That's your truth.

Unfortunately, many of us have told our intuitions to be quiet because those thoughts may not seem practical or logical. Our left brains have convinced us that we must always analyze situations and choose the most perfect logical path that exists on paper. So, we ignore our intuitions even though they are telling us exactly what needs to happen.

IT'S JUST A FEELING

"External circumstances do not create feeling states. Feeling states create external circumstances."
—MARTHA BECK

The best advice on emotions I received was this:

"It's just a feeling."

Who knew that those four words would have such a powerful effect on me? We are always feeling something: happy, sad, tense, afraid, angry, bitter, resentful, joyful, excited, nervous, confident...the list goes on.

When those scary feelings come in, we can get really caught up in them. We let ourselves only think about those feelings and they become worse and worse. Think of a time when you felt overwhelmed with a certain feeling. What happened?

I used to get really caught up in anxious thoughts but never really went over the edge (full panic attack). When I went camping for the first time, it was in Yosemite National Park. I know what you're thinking, who camps in Yosemite for the first time? Well, apparently I like to go big in life.

After hiking over four miles up a mountain, setting up the tent, purifying the water with iodine, and eating the Clif bars (while watching a family cook pasta), the sun started to set. It was time for bed. I fell asleep for about an hour and when I woke up, I was staring through the "moonroof" (what I like to call that see-through mesh at the top of the tent) into blackness.

I started to panic. I was afraid. I thought bears were going to come eat me (there were signs up) and I could barely get myself out of this panicked state. I spent the rest of the evening shaking (it was also very cold at night even though very hot during the day) and praying for the sun to rise.

I wish I knew then what I know now. It was all "just a feeling." While there was a chance of a bear coming, I had taken all the precautions including putting everything that had a scent into the bear canister away from the tent. But I convinced myself that my fear at the moment was real. I was trying to predict the future and I let it take over my entire body. It was a constant fight or flight response that made me exhausted. I realize now that I could have talked myself out of it. How do you do that? Glad you asked.

MANAGING YOUR FEELINGS EXERCISE:

This is the internal dialogue that I would have had with myself during camping. Try filling in your own answers for something happening in your life.

1. What are you feeling?
    Anxious, nervous, scared.

2. What thoughts are making you feel that way?
    The fact that I've been warned that bears are here and will sniff out things that smell if you leave them out and not in the canister. Every sound I hear makes me think there's a bear right outside of this tent.

3. How would you like to feel?
    Comfortable, peaceful, sleepy, one with nature.

4. What can you think to yourself right now to make you feel that way?
    I am safe. I have nothing in my tent that smells. I'm with someone else, not alone. There are other people in tents around here. There is a ranger station close by even though I can't see it. The chance of a bear attacking me is low. Right now, I am okay. Right now, there is no bear here.

See how that works? By thinking those new thoughts, you can get yourself to a better feeling. I do this all the time now when I'm feeling scared or anxious about something. It works.

I actually had the opportunity to practice this recently when I went backpacking through Thailand with my brother. We stayed in bungalows on the jungle island of Koh Chang. These bungalows were built into the hillside in a very deserted part of the island. There were only five people there. On the way to the bungalow at night, while holding a flashlight going down the hill, the man who runs the "resort" told me to watch out for monkeys, scorpions, and snakes. Excuse me?!

Because it's so hot and humid in Thailand, we had to leave the doors to the bungalow wide open. That means that monkeys could easily climb in (at least, that's what the voice in my head was saying). Even though my brother had stayed there before, and even though the man told me the monkeys would not disturb us, I was scared.

But I didn't panic. I may not have had the best sleep, but I didn't let my fear overwhelm me. I was proud of myself for toughing it out and surviving a particularly stressful situation— for four nights.

I haven't only used this exercise in nature and camping scenarios. It is beneficial whenever you feel scared, nervous, angry, tense, or sad about anything: including work situations, tough conversations with your boss, frustrations with friends and family, break-ups or relationship troubles, and even when you are going through a healthy lifestyle change or weight-loss plan. Self-destructive thoughts can happen at any time.

Your thoughts control your feelings. It's up to you how you want to feel.

WHEN EMOTIONS GET STUCK IN YOUR BODY

If you don't experience a feeling, it can become stuck. Feelings and emotions are energy. When you don't release that energy, it stays in your body. Everyone has a different place where this energy becomes stuck, if at all: intestines (stomach ache), muscles (cramps), head (migraines).

When you keep these feelings inside of you, they become suppressed and stay with you. So whenever you experience a similar feeling, your brain will say, "Oh I know this and I don't like it! Therefore, I'm hiding it from you." Your body then suffers. Remember my story in the beginning? Complete suffering. I was hiding feelings that were too painful to remember.

It's important to feel your feelings. Even when they hurt. Even when they suck. Even when they cause you emotional pain. Because if you don't feel them now, they will come back with a vengeance later.

CHAPTER 4

SHIFT YOUR MINDSET & ACHIEVE INNER PEACE

"Worry pretends to be necessary but serves no useful purpose."
—ECKHART TOLLE

Many of us hold back because of fear. Fear of failure, fear of success, fear of embarrassment, fear of being vulnerable. Identifying that fear is what can set you free.

ANXIOUS THOUGHTS

When we say we feel anxious, it usually means we are nervous, scared, or overwhelmed.

We tend to feel anxious before a presentation. Why? Because we fear that we will look like a fool, forget what we are going to say, or not be able to answer any questions.

We feel anxious in our relationships with people. Why? Because we fear they will judge us, analyze us, make fun of us, not like us, or leave us.

We feel anxious when making the decision to quit our jobs and start our own businesses. Why? Because we fear we won't make enough money, that people will judge us, that we won't be supported, or that no one will care.

Does any of this resonate with you? I've felt it all.

It's completely normal to have feelings that make us anxious. What separates those who are happy and calm from those who are overwrought with stress is the ability to identify where the feelings are coming from and flip them around.

HOW TO SHIFT YOUR MINDSET

Identifying the source of your anxiousness is the first step in overcoming it. Remember, we want to dig deep to clarify the feelings you are having. Let yourself be vulnerable. Let's go through this process step-by-step so you can achieve inner peace within a matter of minutes.

SHIFT YOUR MINDSET AND CREATE YOUR MANTRA EXERCISE:

1. Ask yourself, "How am I feeling right now?"
   Think about your real feelings. Overwhelmed? Scared? Angry? Frustrated? Really pay attention and be honest with yourself.

2. Ask yourself, "What is going on in my life that is making me feel this way?"
   These are the thoughts that are making you feel how you responded to the first question. (You may find that some of your thoughts seem absolutely ridiculous once you actually articulate them.)

3. Ask yourself, "How do I want to feel?"
   This should be easy. When I do this exercise, my answers are usually: peaceful, calm, or happy.

4. Ask yourself, "What thought would make me feel this way right now?"
   This is a tough one. It doesn't always come easily. But try to think of something that is true. If you feel like you aren't good enough at your job, your new thought would be, "I am good enough, I do excellent work." If you are very deep into your fears, this may take longer to pull out.

   You can ask yourself, "What is the opposite of my fearful thought?" or "What would my best friend tell me right now if I expressed how I was feeling?"

5. Create a mantra out of your new thought.
   Repeat it to yourself whenever you are feeling stressed again. Write it on a post-it, in your phone, or create a big photograph to hang up. Remember that you can choose to feel differently.

   Your Mantra: _____

As soon as you uncover the deeper feelings and thoughts, sometimes just the awareness of it can make your stress disappear. It's always about feeling better. You may even laugh at yourself for making up such a ridiculous story. Go through the process and see how it works for you. And remember that feelings are just feelings. Once you take away their credibility and power, you regain control.

Creating your mantra around the thoughts and feelings you want to have is your ultimate go-to for when fear-based thoughts come into your brain. When you recite your mantra to yourself over and over, you believe it. Your intuition knows it, but your inner critic (logical left brain) likes to question you about it. Take control and keep your mantra visible at all times. I have created phone wallpapers and post cards for my clients when they find their powerful mantra.

Here are examples of the mantras some of my clients have come up with after doing this exercise.

"I am worth it." (when discussing feelings about her job)

"I can be the woman I want to be." (when discussing feelings about making a lifestyle change)

"I am strong." (when discussing feelings about her illness)

"They are healthy and safe." (when discussing feelings about his children's well-being)

"I deserve to be treated like the wonderful woman I am." (when discussing feelings about her relationship)

"I work better when I'm calm." (when feeling time-stressed with everything she wanted to get done.

CHAPTER 5

EMBRACE THE SECRETS TO EXUDING CONFIDENCE

"When you shine bright your light rubs off on others."
—GABRIELLE BERNSTEIN

SELF-CONFIDENCE vs. SELF-EFFICACY vs. SELF-ESTEEM

They are all very different and it's important to know what they mean.

SELF-CONFIDENCE

Being self-confident is about your competence in a particular skill or thing. Are you good at certain things? Are you competent in a certain area? Your confidence improves as your competence increases.

SELF-EFFICACY

Having self-efficacy is how you judge your competence to complete something. It comes from being confident in a number of things. It's your confidence in your ability to learn. Do you believe you can learn anything you put your mind to?

SELF-ESTEEM

Having self-esteem means you value yourself as a human being. Are you grateful for yourself? Are you in awe of yourself? Do you appreciate the uniqueness you bring to this world?

If you only give value and worth to yourself based on how good you are at something, then you can feel great one day and awful the next.

You are always learning. You are human. You won't ever be excellent at everything. Understanding that makes a much happier person.

You can still feel good about yourself even if you don't run that mile in the time you wanted. Running a mile in a certain amount of time does not affect your value as a human being. You are not just the sum of everything you do. Be kind to yourself. Remind yourself that you are unique; there is only one of you in the world. Celebrate your successes. Celebrate you.

SELF-CONFIDENCE EXERCISE:

To improve self-confidence, practice what you want to be more competent in. Practice the foreign language, run faster, or work on those backbends in yoga class. Keep doing it!

List five skills you want to develop. Then put a star next to the one you are going to start this week.

SELF-EFFICACY EXERCISE:

To improve your self-efficacy, think about everything you've learned in your life. Think about the whole process and how far you've come. Think about the journey, what it took for you to get to that place. Remind yourself that you learned it, that you made it, and that you have the power to continue learning and excelling.

List five learning processes you've taken in your life. Examples: graduating college, learning how to surf, mastering beef bourguignon à la Julia Child.

SELF-ESTEEM EXERCISE:

List five things you love about yourself. Things that make you unique. What makes you feel good about being you?

Keep these lists with you for when you need them. It's very easy to forget about all of the amazing things you have accomplished in your life. When you start to beat yourself up, remember the list. Ask your best friend, parents, or significant other to remind you too. Sometimes hearing it from someone else can really brighten your day and give you the kick you need to continue being your awesome, sexy self.

SELF-CONTROL

"You must give up the life you had planned in order to have
the life that is waiting for you."
—JOSEPH CAMPBELL

We often think we have no control. There are certainly
circumstances where we don't have any control. But we do
have more control than we think. You can always make a
decision. You always have a choice. There are two kinds of
decisions:

Tangible, concrete decisions. E.g., Changing a job, ending a
relationship, moving to a new location.

Intangible, mindful decisions. E.g., Shifting your thinking to
feel better, getting rid of self-destructive thoughts, choosing
to feel calm instead of anxious, happy instead of sad,
accepting instead of fearful. Again, you always have a
choice. You can choose how to feel.

We feel bad and out of control when we face uncertainty
and ambiguity. Some say to embrace these feelings and live in
them because everything in life is this way.

I agree that you should embrace them, but I don't agree
that you should just live in them if they are causing you pain.

Life is uncertain. You never know what will happen. But
you can make decisions now—in your present—to have a more
certain future. You do not have to live in indecision, unless
that's where you want to be. And if you're reading this, it's
likely you don't love the unknown, uncertainty, or ambiguity.
And that's perfectly okay.

Know who you are and accept it. The Type A's, the
perfectionists, the firecrackers...don't change. Adapt based on
what will help you.

As a planner myself, I like to know what's happening. It makes me feel like I have control over the situation, even if I don't, because the feeling is what can make us crazy, not necessarily that we don't have control. So I tried something new. I made a plan to not have a plan. I decided that I didn't need a decision. And it worked.

Tell yourself that you are actually planning to go with the flow or to let something go. In this weird and crazy way, you've just appeased yourself, who you really are, by telling yourself that you will plan to not plan. It's brilliant, and maybe a little sneaky, but it works.

SELF-CONTROL EXERCISE:

Write out something that is making you feel out of control right now. What is bothering you? What do you wish you could do something about? What do you want to take over from someone else? What do you want to plan all alone?

Then think about ways that you do have control. What can you control in the situation? What can you let go of? What really matters?

Is there anything that you can decide to let go of? Decide to ignore? Decide to release the control?

You have to pay attention to your mind and body. If stress and anxiousness are overwhelming you because of the unknown, you have to do something about it. Embracing the unknown—fully living and experiencing each moment— sounds great in theory, and is completely doable when practiced enough, but sometimes we just need a quick fix to calm down our thoughts. This way, you are taking action.

Action can be scary because sometimes we say we don't like uncertainty but it's actually more comfortable than making a decision. Making that decision seems so...final. And finality can be scary. As in life, relationships, and jobs, making the decision is hard. It is frightening. It is concrete. But once you can move past it, the world will open up to you.

CHAPTER 6

INDULGE YOUR MIND, BODY, AND SOUL

"I now see how owning our story and loving ourselves through that process is the bravest thing that we will ever do."
—BRENE BROWN

What does it mean to love yourself?

It can be compared to self-esteem—fully valuing and appreciating all that is you. Loving every part of you. Even the parts that you may doubt.

So how do you do this?

As with self-esteem, celebrate yourself. Pat yourself on the back. Brag to yourself about the things that make you totally awesome. Accept who you are.

SELF-LOVE EXERCISE:

List 10 things you are awesome at and/or things you're proud of yourself for doing this week. Go ahead—I bet you can come up with more than 10.

When you've made the list and feel good about yourself, make a list of things that you want to do, but fear is holding you back from doing them. Nothing is more powerful than conquering a fear.

PLEASURE AND COMFORT

"Both abundance and lack exist simultaneously in our lives, as parallel realities. It is always our conscious choice which secret garden we will tend...when we choose not to focus on what is missing from our lives but are grateful for the abundance that's present—love, health, family, friends, work, the joys of nature and personal pursuits that bring us pleasure—the wasteland of illusion falls away and we experience Heaven on earth."
—SARAH BAN BREATHNACH

Sometimes when we're having a less-than-ideal moment, when we're beating up on ourselves and not loving ourselves, we turn to food. Why? Because we know food (especially the fatty sugary kind) brings us pleasure.

Besides the fact that science tells us that we are chemically wired to crave the fatty, sugary foods, we can't deny that they simply do taste good. Those few seconds of pleasure are what we seek in times of need.

To understand what it really is that is causing this feeling, think about your feelings again. What are you feeling? Are you lonely? Sad? Angry? Avoiding something? Want attention?

Identify what is really happening instead of masking it with food. Maybe you need some love or validation.

Instead of appeasing the pleasure center of your brain with cookies and fries, you can actually access the pleasure center of your brain with what I like to call inedible indulgences.

INEDIBLE INDULGENCES EXERCISE:

This exercise is adapted from one that life coach Martha Beck advises her readers to do. Make a list of the things you love, separated into three categories: people, things, and activities. Put five items in each category.

What brings you pleasure and comfort?

Here are some examples to start you off:
- People: Authors, Friends, Family, TV Characters
- Things: Flowers, Jewelry, Fashion, Cars
- Activities: Kisses, Hugs, Baths, Manicures/Pedicures, Painting, Exercising

Any time you are feeling down on yourself and need an injection of pleasure in your life, go to this list and do something on it. Hug a loved one, read your favorite author, peruse Vogue. You'll get the same amount of pleasure and comfort as you would going for that Junior Bacon Cheeseburger from Wendy's. And you'll actually feel better afterwards.

One of my clients really embraced this and continues using this even after a year. She found herself turning to food, all kinds of food, whenever she was seeking pleasure or comfort. However, she found that going on her favorite website or getting a kiss from her spouse made her feel happier than when she would seek food for pleasure. She's also healthier because of the switch.

CHAPTER 7

FULLY ACCEPT YOUR INNER SEXY

"Only the truth of who you are, if realized, will set you free."
—ECKHART TOLLE

Do you know who you are?

If you do, have you really accepted yourself? It's time to get acquainted with that person. Embrace your flaws and your weaknesses. Admit that you have them. Don't deny it.

For the longest time, I hated feeling jealous. It's an ugly feeling. Every time I felt jealous of someone, I felt myself shrinking on the inside.

One day, a friend said to me that she was very jealous of something I had. She actually used the word jealous, but the way she said it was very loving. I didn't feel threatened or awkward. She was simply stating a fact.

I was so shocked that she admitted that feeling, because I never did. I saw it as a sign of weakness—that I should not think that way at all.

So I started using it. I would admit to myself when I was jealous of someone else and evaluate why. Then I started admitting it out loud to people. I started feeling really good about myself. I was happy that I could be comfortable and confident enough to admit it.

Being jealous slowly morphed into appreciating someone else and what they had rather than feeling down on myself.

Is it an oxymoron to feel good about being jealous? Maybe. But it makes sense. I was being honest. I wasn't hiding feelings. I was being myself.

Once I started admitting it, I either did something about the feeling to get what I wanted or I forgot about it. It's like what I said about releasing emotions and feelings and letting them flow through your body. I experienced my feeling of jealousy. And if it was strong enough, I acted on it. If it wasn't, simply admitting it helped me release the negativity.

Once you admit the jealousy to yourself, reach out to the person you are jealous of. This usually helps you realize that this person is real, just like you. You can usually get some sound advice as well and make a new connection.

Redirecting the energy I was spending feeling jealous— reframing those negative thoughts into positive ones of determination and appreciation—helped me accept myself.

I accept who I am and I know how I want to evolve.

I accept that I don't have everything I want but I believe that I have the ability to get what I want.

I accept my strengths and weaknesses and I know that they make me who I am.

ACCEPTANCE EXERCISE:

Ask yourself these questions:

1. Who are you jealous or envious of right now?

2. What does that person have that you want?

3. Why do you want it?

4. Do you *really* want it?

5. What can you do right now to work towards getting it?

6. What can you tell yourself to feel better about it? (Look at your list of accomplishments.)

STANDING IN YOUR OWN WAY

"If you want a happy ending, that depends, of course, on where you stop your story."
—ORSON WELLES

Honestly, you have the ability to do anything you want. But you are standing in your own way. You need to step aside.

We all have things we want to do. What's stopping us from doing them?

The usual excuses: time and money. But time and money usually have nothing to do with why you aren't doing what you want to do. You can always find the time. You can usually find the money or find a way to do what you want more affordably.

The problem is you. That's right. You. I'm calling you out on it. The reason you aren't doing something you want to do is because:

You really don't want to do it but think you should.

-or-

Some crazy, fictional thought is holding you back from doing it.

Let's take exercising for an example. This may be the thought process going on in your head:

I want to lose weight and tone up. I need to exercise.
But I have no time. When can I go? Before work? Nah, I hate getting up early. After work? Nah, I'm too tired. Plus I'd rather go to happy hour. During lunch? Nah, then I'll be sweaty plus my boss doesn't like it when I leave. Weekends? I'm so tired and busy. Plus I'd rather get drunk at brunch. So I basically have no time.

-or-

I want to lose weight and tone up. I need to exercise. I'll join a gym.
But I have no money. It's so expensive. And what am I going to do when I go there? Take classes? But I'm embarrassed. Everyone is so much more advanced than I am. I'll look like a fool. How will I know what to do when I get there? I don't know what the machines do. I'll feel stupid because everyone else knows what they are doing. And they're already in shape and I'm not. Forget it. I'm not going.

-or-

I want to lose weight and tone up. I need to exercise. But I don't know how.
I'm not in good enough shape to exercise. It won't work. I've tried it before. My body doesn't like it. I don't like to sweat. It's not fun. It sucks. It's a waste of time. I'd rather sit on the couch and watch the Kardashians. Oh look, chocolate chip cookies...

Maybe you have a combination of all three situations running through your head. I certainly have. Let's try to get you to step out of your own head now.

THE SHOULD-ING

> "Courage is the power to let go of the familiar."
> —RAYMOND LINDQUIST

The should-ing is a problem. You think you should exercise, but you really don't want to. Why not?

The time? No. You can always find time, 5 minutes, 10 minutes, 30 minutes. There's always time.

The money? No. You can workout for free in your own home or get discounts on classes and gym memberships.

The actual exercise piece. Yes. This is the problem. You have built up exercising to be this monstrosity of a situation. You have already assumed that you're going to hate it. You also don't know what to do to get the results you want. So you convince yourself that all of these excuses are valid because deep down you don't know what to do and you are afraid of failure.

Those damn thoughts.

SCHEDULING YOUR SELF-SABOTAGING THOUGHTS EXERCISE:

You can use the Scheduling Your Thoughts Exercise I mentioned in Chapter Two to help you deal with these thoughts.

Allot a certain amount of time per day at a particular time to think these thoughts. Whenever you start thinking your irrational thoughts throughout the day, remind yourself that you must wait until the time you've allocated to think them. Then continue doing what you were doing or start doing something else. You'll find as time goes on that you will forget what those thoughts even were. And if you remember them when you've allocated time for them, you'll let yourself think about them, then stop.

When you schedule time during the day to beat up on yourself and feel sorry for yourself, you'll realize how that is a complete waste of time. And if you don't love yourself and treat yourself with respect, who else will?

CHAPTER 8

OWN YOUR EVOLUTION

"The key is to keep company only with people who uplift you,
whose presence calls forth your best."
—EPICTETUS

We are influenced by the people around us. As we evolve
through various stages of life, our interests change. We change.
Naturally, some of our relationships with others don't have the
same impact as before. As you follow your journey through a
lifestyle change, you become very aware of those you want in
your life and those who don't see things as you do. This doesn't
mean you give up friendships, but you may start to evaluate
how much energy and time you put into each relationship.

When you're in this journey, you need like-minded
individuals to inspire you and keep your momentum going.
You've already taken the first step by reading this book.

So, what do you need now?

Accountability. You can have accountability partners, those
who are there to track your progress, keep you motivated, and
ensure that you don't quit. You can also hold yourself
accountable for your own actions (an ideal and advanced
process once you have had some partners).

When this topic arose upon working with Coach Jennie and a virtual coaching group, I realized that I had quite an accountability team in my life among family and friends. But few knew that they were helping me stay accountable for my actions. Just their presence and the fact that we talked often kept me focused. This is "indirect accountability."

"Direct accountability" is when you are specifically checking in with one or more people about progress in a certain area of your life. My clients do this with me as they provide recaps and agendas for all of our coaching sessions every week. They do not want to disappoint me, or themselves, with a lack of progress.

This can work with friends, but both of you really have to want it and be on the same page to hold one another accountable. I have a friend this worked with beautifully (most of the time) when we both worked at our offices in New York and would meet up for gym classes. But we also had our fair share of blowing off the gym to drink wine. I've tried to have other exercise or work accountability partners, but someone usually falls off the wagon.

You really need to hold yourself accountable. Try to find things that will keep you in check.

Whenever I don't do yoga, my body feels it. My body actually gets mad at me and the internal struggle begins. So what do I do? YOGA. I know that I want to do it but that I'm making up excuses. So I do yoga (even for only 10 minutes) and my body thanks me. I hold myself accountable for my own actions and celebrate when I do it.

Bonus: My 12-minute morning yoga routine is on my YouTube channel, plus other popular yoga and exercise videos. YouTube.com/DianaAntholis

Holding yourself accountable is like giving yourself the kick you need to get started again. This may be difficult at first, so I recommend having a partner to keep you going. This works because you don't want to let your partner down or show up for your meeting with nothing done.

I do this with my running group on Facebook, "Runners Unleashed." When I was training for a half marathon, I posted every run and every workout I did. The group posts the workouts they do, but more importantly, they post when they don't feel like going for a run. This is the accountability piece. We cheer one another on to continue toward our goals.

ACCOUNTABILITY EXERCISE:

1. Who are the indirect accountability partners in your life? For me, they are my friends and family.

2. Who are the direct accountability partners in your life? Do you have any? Who would be a good person to start this with? Start small with one project and agree to discuss what you want to accomplish, what day and time you will check-in, and what you will share. If you're a competitive person, this works wonders.

3. What do you want to hold yourself accountable for? What's something you want to be doing but just can't seem to push yourself over the hump to get done as often as you would like? What will make you do it? How do you feel when you do it?

CHAPTER 9

NOURISH YOUR BODY

"As I see it, every day you do one of two things: build health or
produce disease in yourself."
—ADELLE DAVIS

Your diet is 80% of healthy living and feeling good. Exercise
alone won't cut it. You need to eat well while being active. You
are what you eat and you are what you think you eat. Let me
explain.

When it comes to how our body reacts to, processes, and
uses the foods we eat—and what the cells of our bodies are
constructed from—we basically are what we eat. Studies
suggest that we are, actually, what we think we eat.

An ACE Fitness article recently discussed a study done by
Yale University that fed 46 participants the exact same (360
calorie) milkshake and labeled it as either "indulgent" (620
calories) or "health conscious" (140 calories). The participants
consumed each shake one week apart. Researchers measured
the subjects' ghrelin (a hormone that rises to stimulate hunger
when it is time for us to eat) response after each shake was
consumed.

The participants' ghrelin response differed tremendously after each shake despite the fact that they drank the same shake—only the labels (and thus, their perception of each shake) had changed. When participants consumed the "indulgent" shake, their ghrelin levels experienced a significantly steeper decline than when they drank the "health conscious" shake. Thinking they had indulged led them to feel more satisfied for longer (and become hungry later) than when consuming the supposedly healthier shake.

These findings suggest that the psychological mindset of sensibility while eating may actually dampen the effect of ghrelin.

What does this mean? This means that if we believe that a certain food is healthy and therefore consume it, we become hungrier sooner because we believe we ate healthy in the first place. This is a problem when we are deceived by healthy looking non-healthy foods or when we do not know what is healthy and what is not.

I will never say to completely cut out food groups if you don't want to. I will say that I lost 10 pounds by cutting down my meat intake severely. I went from eating meat almost every single day to only once a week. I make sure my meat is organic and I know where it's coming from. I thought I would miss chicken, but I could not care less about it now. Cutting out chicken was easier than cutting out dairy—and dairy was making me sick.

I also don't eat dairy for casein-sensitivity reasons, but will occasionally have some goat or sheep's milk cheese.

My diet mainly consists of legumes, vegetables, fruit, grains (primarily quinoa, sourdough bread, the occasional pasta/rice), and chocolate.

Yes, I said chocolate. I will never deprive you of this luxury! It goes against my core belief—no double D's: dieting and deprivation. Treat yourself. Have a piece of chocolate. Have a cupcake. Just don't eat five in a row every day.

Moderation. (Yes I'm going to use that word.) The idea is to get yourself to a point where you are eating healthfully and deliciously so much that you don't miss that cupcake or ice-cream. In lieu of such sweet treats, have coconut or almond milk ice-cream once in a while. Try sorbet. Make chocolate chip cookie bars out of chickpeas and oats that are healthier for you (recipe on my website). Make burgers out of black beans and sweet potatoes instead of beef. Go out to a restaurant and order something amazing that you have never had before. Indulge. But know when to stop. Know how often to do it. Know when it's hurting your body versus helping it.

Fuel yourself. Take care of yourself. Appreciate this wonderful body that you have. It deteriorates too quickly based on poor choices. You will not lose any tastes. You will not lose any flavors. In fact, you are likely to broaden your palette and likes as you explore foods in new ways. There are options. And I'm here to give them to you.

FOOD SWAPS

One of my clients lost 35 pounds in one year primarily by the food swaps I helped introduce into her diet. She swaps after-dinner cupcakes for fruits like mangos, pineapple, or berries and splits the rare out-to-eat decadent dessert or celebratory birthday cake when she does indulge a bit. After just a couple of weeks, this client noticed that her cravings shifted from the nutritionally-void sugary foods to the healthier snacks.

So, how do you eat healthier without sacrificing taste? This is the most common question I'm asked. That fried, creamy, sugary goodness, which many of us have become addicted to, can cause major health problems (while adding inches to the waistline). Here are five swaps in your daily eating habits that can cut serious calories, fat, and sugar from your diet. And they taste just as good—if not better—than what you are currently eating.

REPLACE HEAVY DESSERTS WITH FRUIT, A CUP OF HERBAL TEA, OR A BIT OF DARK CHOCOLATE

Flour, butter, sugar, heavy cream. These are the main ingredients in those delicious desserts like chocolate cake, croissants, and panna cotta. While I encourage you to treat yourself once in a while to a few bites of an extravagant dessert, eating them often adds unnecessary fat to your diet. (Sugar turns into fat; white carbs turn into fat.)

To tame your sweet tooth, try berries with yogurt, a cup of herbal tea, or a small piece of dark chocolate (the kind that has only a few ingredients). As well as being healthier, you also receive a boost of anti-oxidants. (Bonus: Go to DianaAntholis.com for my Healthy Chocolate Chip Cookie Bar Recipe—you will be shocked by the ingredients and delicious taste. Trust me on this.)

REPLACE COW'S MILK WITH ALMOND, SOY, RICE, OR COCONUT MILK

Cow's milk is very nutritious, as it is provides protein, calcium, and Vitamins A and D (if fortified). However, growing allergies and sensitivities to casein/lactose, extra fat that can be avoided, and higher levels of cholesterol are all good reasons to try a swap. If you must drink cow's milk, skim is the preference; but try something different like unsweetened almond or coconut milk. Even just substituting these in your cereal will make a big difference.

Almond milk is the most nutritious out of the substitutions as it is low in fat and calories, has no cholesterol, and is high in Vitamin E, manganese, magnesium, phosphorous, potassium, selenium, iron, fiber, zinc and calcium. Almond milk also subs in easily for cooking, baking, and even frothing milk for coffee drinks. (Please use caution when sharing almond milk goods with those who have nut allergies.)

REPLACE MAYONNAISE OR BUTTER WITH AVOCADO OR HUMMUS AS A SPREAD

There is hardly any nutritional value to mayonnaise (and it is high in fat and salt), so if you need something to moisten your sandwich, try using spreads of avocado or hummus. Avocado is a healthy fat (the fatty acids in avocados lower cholesterol, promote digestion, and are anti-inflammatory) and provides nearly 20 essential nutrients (including fiber, potassium, Vitamin E, B Vitamins and folate). Hummus is made from chickpeas (garbanzo beans), which are loaded with protein, fiber, and iron, while containing no saturated fat or cholesterol.

REPLACE REGULAR PASTA WITH WHOLE-WHEAT OR BROWN RICE PASTA

White pasta is made from refined white flour, which has no nutritional value. It contains high-glycemic carbohydrates, which means that the sugars from the pasta release into your bloodstream quickly causing a steep rise in your blood sugar levels. Insulin, responsible for regulating sugar in the body, works overtime to even out this spike and turns excess sugar into stored fat. (Hello, diabetes and fat storage around the belly!)

When you eat high-glycemic foods, you may feel a sudden burst of energy but then you crash pretty quickly only to soon feel lethargic and hungry again! The only time high-glycemic foods are recommended is after a vigorous exercise routine since the sugar (glucose) moves into muscles to repair tissue.

Whole-wheat and brown rice have a medium-glycemic index. Foods such as these slowly release sugar into your blood stream—which is optimal—keeping you energetic and full.

REPLACE BUTTER OR OIL IN BAKING WITH
APPLESAUCE

When baking, using applesauce seriously cuts the calories without sacrificing taste. Use the same measurements. If you buy applesauce, buy unsweetened. Even better, make your own applesauce by chopping, boiling, and mashing apples.

BONUS TIP:
EAT PROTEIN INSTEAD OF SUGAR FOR ENERGY

When you need an energy boost, go for protein-rich foods or drinks, not sugar.

A new study shows that protein stimulates the cells responsible for wakefulness and energy. So next time you are tired, skip the candy bars and sugary drinks. Focus on protein-rich foods like egg whites, yogurt, beans, hummus, and nut butters (almond, cashew, peanut, etc.).

FOODS TO EAT EVERY DAY

Want to have optimum nutrition? Here are 12 foods (plus alternative options) that you can eat every day to make sure you are consuming adequate vitamins and minerals. I only give this list out to my Unleash Your Sexy program clients, but it's been so helpful to them that I want to share it with you, as well! Under each food, I explain why it's great to eat it every day, how much of it to have, substitutes that are similar, and meal ideas.

SPINACH

Why?
- Rich source of omega-3s and folate, water-soluble B vitamins (helps reduce risk of heart disease, stroke, osteoporosis) and lutein (fights eyesight degeneration)
- Contains important nutrients: Vitamin A, Vitamin C, Vitamin K, fiber, iron, calcium, potassium, magnesium, and Vitamin E

How much? 1 cup fresh or ½ cup cooked

Substitutes: Other dark green vegetables like Swiss chard, broccoli, kale, bok choy

Meal ideas: Mix in with scrambled eggs, sauté with garlic, add to stir-fry, add to pizza, make a salad.

YOGURT
(plain Greek yogurt, preferably 0% fat)

Why?
- Packed with probiotic organisms, which serve as reinforcements to the beneficial bacteria in your body that help boost your immune system, maintains digestive and intestinal health, and provides protection against cancer (make sure label says "live and active cultures")
- Rich in calcium, phosphorus, potassium, zinc, riboflavin, Vitamin B12, and protein

How much? 1 cup

Meal ideas: Top with berries, nuts, cinnamon, honey. Make healthier dips and salad dressings using yogurt as a base (in lieu of sour cream or mayo…Greek yogurt makes a great base for a healthy-but-still-delicious dips).

RED TOMATOES

Why?
- Contains the antioxidant lycopene, which decreases risk of bladder, lung, prostate, skin, and stomach cancers as well as reduces the risk of coronary artery disease

How much? 1 tomato, 8 cherry, or 1 glass of tomato juice

Substitutes: Red watermelon, pink grapefruit, papaya, guava

Meal ideas: Add into eggs, salads, and stir-fry dishes. Make tomato sauce or drink tomato juice.

BLUEBERRIES

Why?
- Contain the most antioxidants of any other North American fruit, help prevent cancer, diabetes, and age-related memory changes, and boost cardiovascular health
- Rich in fiber and Vitamins A and C

How much? 1 cup fresh, ½ cup frozen or dried

Substitutes: Açai berries, purple grapes, prunes, raisins, strawberries, cranberries

Meal ideas: Add to yogurt, oatmeal, salads, or eat alone or as a jam (no added sugar).

CARROTS

Why?
- Contain carotenoids, fat-soluble compounds that are associated with the reduction in a wide range of cancers as well as reduced risk and severity of inflammatory conditions such as asthma and rheumatoid arthritis
- Low caloric density
- Great source of beta-carotene and Vitamin A

How much? ½ cup

Substitutes: Sweet potato, pumpkin, butternut squash, yellow bell pepper, mango (think: orange)

Meal ideas: Eat raw carrots plain or with dips (hummus, yogurt dip), add to soups, and chop up into to a stir-fry.

BLACK BEANS

Why?
- Full of anthocyanins, an antioxidant compound that has been shown to improve brain function
- Packed with protein and fiber (8 grams protein, 7.5 grams soluble fiber per serving)
- Low in calories and NO saturated fat
- Good source of iron (pair with sweet potatoes, lemon juice, or other Vitamin C rich food to boost iron absorption)

How much? ½ cup

Substitutes: Pinto, kidney, fava, and lima beans, peas, lentils, garbanzo beans (chickpeas)

Meal ideas: Wrap in a breakfast burrito, add to chili, make into a dip, add to salsa, eat with rice, add in a stir-fry.

WALNUTS

Why?
- Richer in omega-3s than salmon—2.5 grams of omega-3s per one serving (1 ounce/7 whole nuts) of walnuts vs. 2 grams per one serving (3 ounces) of salmon
- Highest amount of the ALA (alpha linoleic acid) omega-3 fat {vs. EPA (eicosapentaenoic acid) and DHA (docosahexaenoic acid) found in salmon} The American Heart Association recommends 11 grams of ALA per week
- High mono- and polyunsaturated-fat content helps reduce total and "bad" LDL cholesterol levels while maintaining "good" HDL cholesterol
- Has more anti-inflammatory polyphenols than red wine
- Has half as much muscle-building protein as chicken
- Great post-workout recovery snack

How much? 1 ounce (7 whole nuts)

Substitutes: Almonds, peanuts, pistachios, macadamia nuts, hazelnuts

Meal ideas: Add to yogurt, granola bars, salads, or eat plain.

OATS

Why?
- First food to get FDA approval for heart-disease prevention potential
- Contain soluble fiber, which lowers blood cholesterol and protects against heart disease. Oats also help regulate your digestive system.
- Complex carbs, because of their high protein content (10 grams per serving), slow down the release of sugar into the blood stream, making it possible for you to use the fuel as energy and to build muscle

How much? ½ cup

Substitutes: Quinoa, flaxseed, wild rice

Meal ideas: Add fruit for breakfast, make granola bars, sprinkle ground flaxseed on cereal, salad, yogurt, and in baking, and use quinoa for breakfast or dinner bases.

EGGS

Why?
- High-quality protein
- Eat egg whites if watching your cholesterol and trying to lose weight

How much? 1 egg

Meal ideas: Add scrambled eggs to burritos, hard-boiled eggs to salads, and make omelets for breakfast or dinner.

APPLES

Why?
- Contain insoluble and soluble fiber (they are filling plus reduce cholesterol)
- Reduce the risk of heart disease
- Chewing apples stimulates saliva, which scrubs stains off your teeth and freshens your breath
- Low calorie

How much? 1 apple

Meal ideas: Eat plain (as a snack when you are on the go), sliced with nut butter, or baked (with a sprinkle of cinnamon).

SWEET POTATOES

Why?
- Contain alpha and beta carotene, which your body converts to Vitamin A that keeps your eyes, bones, and immune system healthy and they operate as antioxidants
- One ½ cup serving (one medium sweet potato) provides four times the recommended daily value of Vitamin A, plus some Vitamin C and B6, potassium, manganese, lutein, and zeaxanthin
- It is one of the most nutritious vegetables in the land

How much? ½ cup (one medium sweet potato)

Meal ideas: Bake them whole or sliced, add to burritos, include in a stir-fry or omelet…eat sweet potatoes at any time of the day!

ORANGES

Why?
- Excellent source of Vitamin C, which is critical for producing white blood cells and antibodies that fight off infections, and a powerful antioxidant that helps protect cells from free-radical damage and plays a key role in producing collagen
- High in fiber and folate

How much? 1 large orange or 1 cup of orange juice (100% juice)

Meal ideas: Add into salads, eat plain (another great on-the-go snack), use the juice for home-made salad dressings or smoothies.

FOODS TO EAT EVERY WEEK

The following 12 foods are packed with vitamins, minerals, and antioxidants. Feel free to have them anywhere from 3 to 7 times per week.

What are antioxidants? Plant foods are good for you and they produce chemicals called antioxidants. They help protect your cells against oxidation (think of oxidation as rust). This cellular rust is caused by free radicals, which are unstable oxygen atoms that attack your cells, inducing DNA damage that can lead to cancer. Antioxidants help stabilize free radicals, which keeps the atoms from harming your cells.

By eating more antioxidant-rich foods, you'll boost the amount of the disease-fighting chemicals floating in your bloodstream. The result: every bite fortifies your body with all-natural preventive medicine.

WHOLE GRAINS

Why?
- Rich source of fiber
- Essential for muscle building

How much? 1 cup

Examples: quinoa, wild rice, whole wheat, oats, pastas, and cereals

Meal ideas: Use in a stir-fry, a side dish with sauce, oats for breakfast or dressed up with baked apples for dessert.

BEETS

Why?
- Great source of folate and betaine, which work together to lower blood levels of homocysteine, an inflammatory compound that can damage your arteries and increase your risk of heart disease

How much? 1 cup

Meal ideas: Eat fresh, roasted, or sautéed. Add cooked or raw beets to salads for a healthy and pretty boost to your greens.

CINNAMON

Why?
- May help control blood sugar and cholesterol (which helps reduce your risk of heart disease) Methylhydroxychalcone polymers increase your cells' ability to metabolize sugar by up to 20 times

How much? 1 teaspoon

Meal ideas: Add to oatmeal, baked apples, yogurt, coffee or cider.

POMEGRANATE JUICE

Why?
- Lowers blood pressure and is loaded with antioxidants

How much? 1 cup

Meal ideas: Drink with breakfast, add to smoothies, use as a flavorful base for salad dressings.

PUMPKIN SEEDS

Why?
- Packed with magnesium, which is associated with a lower risk of early death

How much? ¼ cup

Meal ideas: Eat these roasted or raw sprinkled into salads, granola, and trail mixes.

GUAVA

Why?
- Higher concentration of lycopene (an antioxidant that fights prostate cancer) than tomatoes or watermelon and one cup provides 688 milligrams of potassium (63% more than in a medium banana)
- High fiber food, 9 grams in every cup

How much? 1 whole guava

Meal ideas: Eat fresh, frozen, added into smoothies, or cut up into a tropical fruit salad.

GOJI BERRIES

Why?
- Have the highest ratings in gauging antioxidant power of any fruit
- High in protein with 18 amino acids
- Only 35 calories per tablespoon

How much? ¼ cup

Meal ideas: Add into smoothies, eat fresh, add dried berries to oatmeal, trail mix, or yogurt.

KIWIS

Why?
- As one of the most nutritionally dense foods, one kiwi provides your daily requirement for Vitamin C
- Good source of potassium and fiber
- Decent source of Vitamin A and Vitamin E

How much? 1 kiwi

Meal ideas: Eat fresh, add to fruit salad, or make a little frozen dessert by dipping slices into dark chocolate and freezing individual servings.

QUINOA

Why?
- One of the best whole grains you can eat
- High protein (8 grams in one cup cooked)
- High fiber (5 grams per cup)
- Contains zinc, Vitamin E, iron, and selenium

How much? 1 cup

Meal ideas: Use in place of rice or create cold salads with beans, veggies, and different dressings.

AVOCADO

Why?
- Healthy monounsaturated fat (lower cholesterol, promote digestion, and anti-inflammatory)
- Provides nearly 20 essential nutrients (i.e. fiber, potassium, Vitamin E, B-Vitamins & folate)

How much? ¼ of a medium avocado

Meal ideas: Eat fresh with a squeeze of lime juice and sprinkle of sea salt, make into fresh guacamole, and add to sandwiches as a healthy spread.

SALMON

Why?
- High in protein
- High in omega-3 fats that help fat-burning, not fat-storing
- Highest amount of omega-3 fats EPA (eicosapentaenoic acid) and DHA (docosahexaenoic acid) at 2 grams per serving

How much? Eat once a week (One 3 oz. serving = roughly the size of an iPhone)

Meal ideas: Grill, bake, or steam with some lemon. Experiment with using cedar plank or different herbs for flavoring.

WINTER SQUASH

Why?
- Provides 170% of daily requirement of Vitamin A (necessary for night vision)
- High in carotenoids, antioxidants for eyesight
- L-tryptophan, which can help to prevent depression
- Rich source of magnesium, which will lower your risks for heart disease, abdominal obesity, and diabetes.

How much? 1 cup

Meal ideas: Try as a soup base, with roasted vegetables, or as ravioli filling (in place of cheese).

SERVINGS PER DAY

Here are the servings you should be eating every day to be healthy and to better manage your weight:

Grains: 7-8 servings per day (servings are ½ cup to 1 cup)

Vegetables: 4-5 servings per day (servings are ½ cup to 1 cup)

Fruits: 4-5 (servings are ½ cup to 1 cup)

Low-fat dairy: 2-3 (1 cup)

Meats: 2 or less (3 oz. which is roughly the size of an iPhone)

Nuts, seeds, dry beans: 4-5 per week (servings are: ½ cup nuts, 2 tbsp. seeds, ½ cup dried beans)

Fats and oils: 2-3 (1 tsp. extra virgin olive oil, 2 tbsp. light dressing)

Sweets: limit to maximum of 5 per week (1 tbsp. of something sweet like candy, jam, or other processed sugars)

LISTEN TO YOUR BODY

Much of the mind-body work we've done in this workbook can help with your digestion, if you are noticing problems there. At age 20, I realized that stress was completely messing up my intestines.

More and more people I talk with are having this problem. They're afraid to talk about it because digestive issues can be incredibly embarrassing. It's a sensitive subject, so not many people talk about it unless I specifically ask questions and tell my story. They go to doctors; they are put on medications; they are told to get more sleep.

However, if there is nothing structurally wrong with you, the problem is usually stress. You have to identify what's stressing you out and flip your mind around.

Yes sleeping more, eating healthier, meditating, exercising, and relaxing help this. Absolutely. But your mind is powerful. Your thoughts are powerful. And they can control your body. You need to get out of the negative cycle and into a positive one.

Stomach pain is a common issue. When you start to get stomach pain, talk to yourself. Ask yourself how you are feeling. Ask yourself why you are feeling that way. Identify the thought. Bring awareness to it. Usually, as soon as you realize the problem, it can disappear. Go through the Shift Your Mindset Exercise in Chapter Four that we did earlier to see how you can talk yourself down from high-stress thoughts.

Digestive discomfort happened to me whenever I was nervous. I would feel queasy and have pain. I usually let it overwhelm me.

That's not healthy. I understood that my stress was unhealthy but I didn't know how to fix it. You have to identify the cause of your anxiousness and then think about how you would rather feel.

Once you figure out what is causing you to have that particular feeling, you can start thinking of things that will make you feel better. Whenever this happens to me, I tell myself that I want to feel calm and in control. I remind myself that I actually have complete control.

And almost like magic, my pain goes away. My body calms down. It was all because of my thoughts. Try it next time.

CHAPTER 10

FALL IN LOVE WITH MOVEMENT

"People tend to think of breakthroughs in medicine as a new drug, a laser, or a high-tech surgical procedure. They often have a hard time believing that the simple choices that we make in our lifestyle—what we eat, how we respond to stress, whether or not we smoke cigarettes, how much exercise we get, and the quality of our relationships and support—can be as powerful as drugs and surgery. And they often are."
—DEAN ORNISH, M.D.

We've talked about how to get our minds in shape and how to eat better. Now it's time for shaping our bodies. Once you've identified what's holding you back, you can begin to move forward with the exercising piece. But it won't work if you don't give your mind a good workout first. You may start strong, but it will fade. It happens to the best of us. You know how great you feel when you're happy and in a good mood. You feel like you can conquer the world. Starting an exercise program is no different. You have to be ready to commit in order to get the results you want.

It's true that it can take 4 weeks for you to notice a change in your body, 8 weeks for friends and family to notice, and 12 weeks for the world to notice.

Don't give up. My clients have noticed changes in even less time when they really stick to their goals. It helps you stay committed to every workout.

It's also true that you should do workouts that you enjoy, not that you dread. You need to want to do it in order to actually do it. Try new classes: yoga, kickboxing, Zumba, etc. Find something you love. Stick with it.

The way you stick to exercising consistently is accountability. As I said earlier, holding yourself accountable is the best, but when starting out, use others directly and indirectly to keep you going. I know many who are training to run races and need that extra push from others to keep going (or just knowing that others are there for them and doing the same thing).

YOUR FITNESS PERSONALITY

There are times when you just don't feel like moving your body. The couch is calling your name. Happy hour is too good to resist. Your boss has convinced you to stay late. Whatever it is, we've all experienced it.

This is why I created MOOD workouts. These are workouts that you plan based on your potential future mood. You know yourself better than anyone. Choose workouts based on the moods you are in.

Some examples:

- The "There's no freaking way I'm opening my eyes right now" Workout

- The "I need to smash something Hulk-style right now" Workout

- The "Need wine. Need chocolate. Need bed now." Workout

Sound familiar?

Pick out your typical moods (tired, hungry, angry, lazy, have 10-minutes until I have to be in the shower) and then write down the workouts for each mood. My coaching clients and I have fun with these until we perfect the workout that really goes with that mood.

When you are insanely tired but want to move your body a little bit, do one minute of your favorite exercise. Bicycle abs, push-ups, squat kicks. It doesn't matter what it is, just move.

When you are extremely frustrated and need to expend your extra energy, do your favorite hard-core 45-minute workout. Kick it, punch it, push it, jump it. Let it all out.

When you really just want to lie on the couch and drink wine, do a few sun salutations and downward dogs to breathe life back into your body. Get the blood flowing and breathe deep.

Why do we do this? To form a habit. If you get in the habit of moving your body—even just the slightest—every day, then exercising comes naturally. Your body will crave exercise.

MOOD WORKOUTS EXERCISE:

Pick out 4 of your most common moods and choose workouts to fit those moods.

What's the point of this? It gets you in the habit of moving your body every single day, no matter how glued-shut your eyes are, how much tequila you drank the night before, or how much your boss ticked you off.

Then you will actually crave moving, sweating, and feeling the air fill up your lungs.

WORKOUTS IN 30 MINUTES OR LESS

Since time is such a factor in all of our lives, I've designed effective workouts that can be done in 30 minutes that give you all you need to burn fat and tone up. Follow the links below to exclusive videos I made just for you.

Here is the website address for your private videos: http://dianaantholis.com/unleashedprivatevideos

Password: unleashed2013

When you land on the private page and enter the password, you will see two workouts to click on: Lean & Sexy Workout link and the Sculpt & Tone Workout link. Each video is designed to open up in a webpage. Then get started!

UNLEASH YOUR SEXY WORKOUT VIDEOS

Want downloadable, targeted, short workouts? The Unleash Your Sexy Workout Videos are available for download. Here's why you need them in your life:

FULL DOWNLOAD. So you can keep it on your computer, tablet, or phone forever and never have to worry about your Internet connection ruining your workout again.

INTENSITY IN A SHORT AMOUNT OF TIME. The average length is 12 minutes.

TARGET THE SPOTS YOU WANT TO WORK ON THE MOST. Thighs, hips, arms, back, core, butt. I got you covered.

NO EQUIPMENT OR GYM NECESSARY. You use your own bodyweight the entire time. You can do these videos ANYWHERE.

COMPLETE WORKOUT. I know you're super busy, so follow along as I workout with you.

RELAX WITH A GUIDED MEDITATION. For one minute after your workout, you lie down and listen to my (incredibly calming) voice guide you into relaxation, fully appreciating the workout you just did.

A SPOTIFY MUSIC PLAYLIST. To pump you up during your workout.

When you select the package with all of the workout videos, you also receive a training calendar to follow.

You can find these workout videos here: dianaantholis.com/workout-videos

CONCLUSION

"If you do not change direction, you may end up where you are heading."
—LAO-TZU

You can lead the balanced, centered, and sexy life you deserve. In reading this book, you have already committed yourself to living a healthier and happier life.

Thank you for listening to my story. I love that I can share this information with you so you can start living your best life immediately.

This journey isn't always easy, but it's worth it. It took me nearly 10 years to understand the connection between my mind and body. It took years of research, experimenting, and talking to others. It took courage. It took perseverance. It took patience (something I don't have copious amounts of naturally). It took accountability.

It is not easy to bring your thoughts, feelings, and emotions out of hiding. We have been conditioned as a society to hide our feelings, stuff down our emotions, and show that we are tough—that we don't let anything get to us.

For those who struggle to find balance, remember that your peace of mind is waiting for you to take action. It's about defining it, prioritizing it, and taking time for yourself.

For those who feel as though you are swirling around life and want to find your center, take a deep breath and remember your mantra. Ask yourself how you are feeling. Think thoughts that make you feel good. Don't let fear and stress take over your thoughts.

For those who want to unleash your sexy, you have to believe that you have it in you first. Remember that you have control—more than you may think. Love yourself, accept yourself, and unleash your true self to the world.

Eat in moderation, try tasty alternatives, and get your vitamins from real food. Move your body for at least 30 minutes per day—whether you use my workout videos, go for a walk, or try a new dance class. Find an accountability partner; then, start holding yourself accountable.

I use the exercises in this book every time I need them. In fact, I needed them as I was writing the book! Having some starting points for inspiration really does help get you moving.

If I were to leave you with only a few thoughts, it would be these:

Only you can make yourself happy—not anything
or anyone else can.

You are not your thoughts. You can change your thoughts.

Feel your feelings, no matter what. Cry, laugh,
or scream when you need to.

You can make a change in your lifestyle. Start small.
Watch the progress. Have patience. Enjoy the benefits.

The thoughts you send out into the world are the ones that
come true—make them count.

Here's to living your balanced, centered, and sexy life.

UNLEASH YOUR SEXY

Sexy is when you feel good about you.
Your mind. Your body. Your being.

Sexy is enjoying life. Feeling good. Staying centered.

Sexy is genuine happiness. When you smile because life is good.
When you appreciate the abundance in your life.

Sexy is when you stop planning, worrying, and over-thinking.
It's when you let it happen, when you let it flow.

Sexy is accepting that you are beautiful, strong, and capable.

Sexy is when you've made the ever-important decision to
accept yourself—no matter what.

Unleashing your sexy is a mindset. It's being you.

If UNLEASHED has transformed the way you think about
your mind and body, I'd love to hear from you. Write to me at
diana@dianaantholis.com

I'd love to have you join the Unleash Your Sexy Community.
It's free. DianaAntholis.com/membership

Join me online. I'm the only Diana Antholis in the world,
which means I rank on the first page of Google.

EXERCISES LIST

ACKNOWLEDGEMENTS

I am so grateful for the beautiful people in my life.

My parents: much love for the endless support, the edits, and acting as my publicity team.

My brother Steven: a huge thank you for beautifully designing the front and back covers of this book, filming my exercise videos, making the graphics on my website, and leading me through Thailand for a month.

Guillaume: thank you for always listening, the advice, the support, the love, and for making me feel like the most beautiful person in the world.

My best girlfriends: thank you for the support, the wine, the adventures, and acting as editors and creative directors.

My editor, Amie Montemurro: thank you for editing this book, believing in my cause, and loving grammar.

The entrepreneurs, bloggers, and coaches I've met along the way: thank you for the support, the accountability, and the "blind date meetings."

The Unleash Your Sexy community: I could not have done this without you. You are beautiful people who deserve to live your best lives. Thank you for accompanying me on this journey.

ABOUT THE AUTHOR

As a Lifestyle-ist, Mind Body Specialist, and American Council on Exercise Certified Personal Trainer, Diana Antholis shows women how to lead the balanced, centered, and sexy lives they deserve. She is the founder of DianaAntholis.com and the creator of the Unleash Your Sexy Program.

Diana takes the mind, body, and soul approach to health and happiness—inspiring and changing women's lives. After coaching and training with Diana, her clients have felt rejuvenated, stronger (on the inside and out), and ready to take charge of their lives.

Diana's philosophy is to help women fall in love with movement, eat healthfully with indulgences, achieve inner peace, be in the present moment, and embrace their inner sexiness.

Her background in corporate advertising, management consulting, and higher education led her to experience first-hand the physical and mental stress occurring in the workplace. As she developed her own tools and resources to live a more balanced, centered, and sexy life, she left the corporate lifestyle to help others navigate their own lives in such stressful environments. She realized that you have to create your own happiness because no one else will do it for you.

Diana's master's degree is in Organizational Management from The George Washington University in Washington D.C. Her bachelor's degree is in Advertising and Marketing Communications from the Fashion Institute of Technology in NYC.

She is always pursuing additional health certifications, specifically in yoga instruction and nutrition.

From central New Jersey, Diana has lived, worked, and studied in Manhattan, San Diego, and Washington D.C. She plays tennis, practices yoga, runs, skis, swims, and likes to challenge herself with ambitious goals like running a half marathon and completing a triathlon. Diana loves to create and share delicious and healthy recipes, while also perfecting her chocolate-chip cookies. Follow her on social media for inspirational tweets, centering status updates, chocolate recipe pins, travel photos, and yoga videos.

30822730R00064

Made in the USA
Lexington, KY
19 March 2014